S is for Sunshine
A Florida Alphabet

Written by Carol Crane and Illustrated by Michael Glenn Monroe

Sleeping Bear Press
310 North Main Street
P.O. Box 20
Chelsea, MI 48118
www.sleepingbearpress.com

Printed and bound in Canada.

10 9 8 7 6 5 4 3 2

Library of Congress Cataloging-in-Publication Data

Crane, Carol, 1933-
S is for sunshine : a Florida alphabet / author, Carol Crane ;
illustrator, Michael Glenn Monroe
p. cm.

ISBN 1-58536-012-0
1. Florida—Juvenile literature. 2. English
language—Alphabet—Juvenile literature. [1. Florida—Miscellanea. 2.
Alphabet.] I. Monroe, Michael (Michael G.), ill. II. Title.
F311.3 .C73 2000
917.59—dc21
00-009984

For Conrad and our seven grandsons:
Brad, Bryan, Blair, Pat Jr., Paul,
Conner, and Casey...all readers.

Carol Crane

To my sister, Jane, also an artist, her husband,
Bruce, and my two nephews, Ryan and Joey.
Thanks for all of your support.

Michael Glenn Monroe

A is for Alligator,
a slow submarine with eyes.
Brackish water, swamps, and rivers,
on the banks he lies.

The alligator is our state reptile. This reptile has lots of teeth, but cannot chew. Teeth are used to grab food and then it is swallowed whole. A mother alligator lays 20-50 eggs into a nest, called a clutch. An alligator can stay underwater for more than an hour. On land, the alligator can only run in a straight line. It is the largest reptile in North America.

Beach sands are different colors in Florida. White sand is made of quartz. Tan sand is broken pieces of colored shells. Black sand, unusual for Florida, is caused by minerals.

Florida is a peninsula. A peninsula is land that is almost surrounded by water. The Atlantic Ocean is east of Florida. The Straits of Florida is to the south and east. The Gulf of Mexico lies to the west and to the south. The states of Alabama and Georgia are to the north.

B is for Beaches,
700 miles of shells and sand.
Tiny little crystals,
sifting through my hand.

Florida is the largest cattle grazing state east of the Mississippi River. The subtropical climate grows grass for the cattle all year long. "Cracker" is another name for cowboy, who with the snap of his cracking whip, drives the cattle.

When the Spanish arrived in Florida, they brought with them the first Florida cattle. Cattle living in Florida have to be able to withstand subtropical heat and humidity. The Brahman, imported from India via Texas, have large humps on their backs. Another breed of cattle seen in the Florida grazing fields are Texas Longhorns. Why do you think they are called Longhorns?

Coreopsis is the state wild flower and can be found throughout Florida.

C is for cattle, crackers, and cowboys, working in the saddle. Cowboys cracking their whips, miles of grazing cattle.

The dolphin is also called a porpoise. Florida has adopted the dolphin as the official saltwater mammal. The dolphin has keen eyesight, a wonderful sense of hearing, and makes a variety of sounds. If you tap on the side of your boat, dolphins will often come to see what is making this noise. Sailors believe if dolphins jump or circle around their boats, it is a sign of good luck.

The Florida Legislature adopted the sailfish as the official saltwater fish. This fish swims very fast, often up to speeds of 60 mph.

D is for Dolphin,
dancing around my boat.
Diving, jumping just for me,
dolphin play is fun to see.

The Everglades, a natural treasure of Florida, is the largest remaining subtropical wilderness in the United States. It is the home to many birds, alligators, panthers, snakes, fish, and turtles. Water flows through the glades at about one-half mile per day.

The Florida Panther is our state's official animal. It is a large cat, six feet or longer, long tailed, and pale brown. It is on the endangered list.

Everglades starts with E,
a grassy river that runs to the sea.
A glade is an open place in nature,
Native Americans call it "Pa Hay Okee".

In 1868, the official flag was designed. It bore the state seal on a field of white. The state seal has a brilliant sun, a large Sabal Palm tree, a steamboat sailing on sparkling waters, and a Native American woman scattering flowers. In 1900, the red diagonal bars were added.

The Sabal Palm is the official tree of Florida. It helped the early settlers in three ways. The young buds were eaten, the trunks were used to build log cabins and forts, and the fronds were used for thatched roofs.

GREAT SEAL OF THE STATE OF FLORIDA

IN GOD WE TRUST

Ff

F is for the Florida Flag,
adopted in eighteen sixty-eight.
Official emblem of our state,
we honor our flag, it's great!

G is for Gardens,
fruits, vegetables, and flowers.
All the rainbow colors,
bathing in sun and showers.

Watermelons, strawberries, grapefruit, oranges, corn, tomatoes, and beans are a few of the plant crops grown in Florida. Everywhere you look there are beautiful flowers growing. Poinsettias and Easter Lilies are seen growing in large fields. All of these fruits, vegetables, and plants are found in markets all across the nation.

H is for the Horse Conch,
a colorful shell to see.
Natives once used it
to call from key to key.

The Horse Conch is the official state shell of Florida. Shell hunters love to discover this beautiful large, orange shell. It is found in sandy grass flats, for here is where the Horse Conch finds the food he needs to survive. In March, there is a conch shell horn-blowing contest, held in the Florida Keys.

H h

I is for Inventor,
a man of great fame.
He invented the light bulb,
do you know his name?

Thomas Alva Edison lived in Ft. Myers, Florida in the winter. He had a laboratory and worked on many projects there. His next-door neighbor was Henry Ford of automobile fame. Mr. Edison did many experiments on the goldenrod plant, from which he produced rubber for tires. Mr. Edison loved plants and was given an India Banyan tree, which he planted outside his laboratory. It is one of the largest trees of its kind in Florida.

Ii

Juan Ponce de León was an explorer and adventurer. He was sent from Spain to look for gold and to claim land for King Ferdinand. He landed in Puerto Rico and found rich gold deposits there. He again sailed to explore other areas, looking for the Fountain of Youth, and landed on Easter Sunday, 1513 in what we now call St. Augustine. He called this new land La Florida, meaning "land of flowers." Spain's Eastertime celebration is called "Pascua Florida" (feast of the flowers).

J is for Juan Ponce de León,
an explorer of old.
He discovered Florida,
while searching for gold.

The Overseas Highway connects the many islands in the Florida Keys, starting at Miami and ending at Key West. The clear waters surrounding the islands are a beautiful emerald green, providing the best place to see over 650 different species of brightly colored fish. Over thousands of years, coral reefs have been made from the skeletons of tiny sea creatures. Molded together, the hard, stony coral has formed reefs. These reefs, along Florida's coastline, are very fragile and are protected by the State of Florida.

Key Deer are only found in the Florida Keys. Weighing only 50 to 80 pounds, and standing 2 feet tall, they are often called "toy" deer.

Now **K** is for the Keys,
a coral necklace in the sun.
Riding over bridges,
counting islands one by one.

L is for Lake Okeechobee.
How do Seminoles say this name?
"Oki" is big, and "Chobi" is water,
a levee has made it tame.

Lake Okeechobee is the largest freshwater lake in Florida and the second largest in the United States. It is noted for its great fishing and importance to the Everglades. The Lake Okeechobee Scenic Trail rims the Herbert Hoover Dike, a 115-mile structure built to contain the lake. This walking and biking trail provides great views of citrus groves, sugarcane fields, and historic communities.

The official Florida State Freshwater Fish is the Largemouth Bass. It is not uncommon to catch a Largemouth Bass that weighs 20 pounds!

Ll

M is for Mockingbird,
whose songs fill the air.
He copies the other birds,
but he doesn't care.

The Mockingbird is the state bird of Florida. He sings day and night, repeating the songs of other birds three to six times. The eggs of the mockingbirds are a beautiful light blue with soft brown spots. Sandhill Cranes, Wood Storks, Roseate Spoonbills, Pelicans, Great White Heron, and Flamingos are all long-legged birds that can be seen along waterways or open grasslands in Florida.

M
m

NASA is the National Aeronautics and Space Administration. The John F. Kennedy Space Center and NASA are located on Merritt Island National Wildlife Refuge. These space centers carefully share the area with 500 different varieties of endangered birds, mammals, reptiles, and amphibians. What an awesome sight!

In 1970, the Florida lawmakers designated the Moonstone as the state gem. This was to honor the first manned flight to land on the moon. Oddly enough, the moonstone is not found on the moon, nor is it native to Florida.

N n

N is for NASA,
rockets lifting into space.
Man and nature sharing
God's earth with grace.

Spanish explorers planted the first orange trees around St. Augustine, Florida between 1513 and 1565. Today, Florida is the second largest producer of oranges in the world, following Brazil. Every day 540 truckloads of oranges are received at Tropicana, where 50 million oranges are processed each day. Every minute, juice is extracted from 700 oranges.

Orange Blossom starts with O,
the fragrance is so sweet.
It is the state flower of Florida,
and the fruit is good to eat.

Shipwrecks caused by hurricanes
and pirate attacks on Spanish
ships, heavy with treasures, have
sunk off the coasts of our state.
Some of their treasures, such as
gold coins, have washed up on
the beaches of Florida.

P
is for Pirates,
raiding Spanish ships for gold.
Sunken ships, buried treasure,
stories of adventure told.

Q is for Queen Angelfish,
colorful as can be.
Swims right up to my mask,
a stunning sight to see.

Swimming in the coral reefs are many beautiful fish. One fish, the Queen Angelfish, is shy around swimmers but is also very curious, sometimes swimming right up to the masks of people snorkeling. Fish swim in groups called schools.

Ringling Brothers, and Barnum & Bailey Circus had their winter headquarters in Sarasota, Florida. There is a circus museum there to honor John Ringling.

Located in the same area is The John and Mable Ringling Museum of Art, one of the finest art collections of its kind. It was given to the State of Florida.

R is for John Ringling,
a man who loved the circus.
Lions, tigers, elephants, and clowns,
high wire acrobats, glittery gowns.

S is for St. Augustine,
where a coquina fort was erected.
So our nation's oldest city
and its settlers were protected.

The fort in St. Augustine was built to last over 300 years. Through history, the Castillo De San Marcos has been attacked many times but never conquered. The walls of the fort are made from coquina, a porous limestone formed a million years ago from the coquina clam. The fort was declared a National Monument in 1924.

St. Augustine is also home to the U.S.'s oldest wooden school-house, oldest house, and oldest lighthouse.

Now we have an important letter,
I hope you will agree.
It is the capital of our state:
T is for Tallahassee.

All of the rules and laws of our state are made and voted on by our representatives, senators and our governor who work in our capitol. Our capitol is rich in history. Three log cabins served as the first capitol. As Florida grew, a new domed capitol was built and many additions for new offices have been added throughout the years.

Tallahassee is located in the panhandle of Florida. Can you find the panhandle on a map?

U

Underwater Aquarium starts with U,
watching shapes all day.
Turtles, exotic fish, and manatee,
dancing a water ballet.

There are many places in Florida where you can swim with the fish, watch the manatee, or see the variety of turtles drifting slowly about. The show is always different. The manatee is the official marine mammal of Florida and has been called the gentle sea cow. The loggerhead turtle is one of many varieties of turtles to view; both are protected so that we may watch them forever.

U u

Millions of visitors come to the
Sunshine State each year. Some come
for a short visit, others come to stay.

Vis for Vacationers,
that come for sun and pleasure.

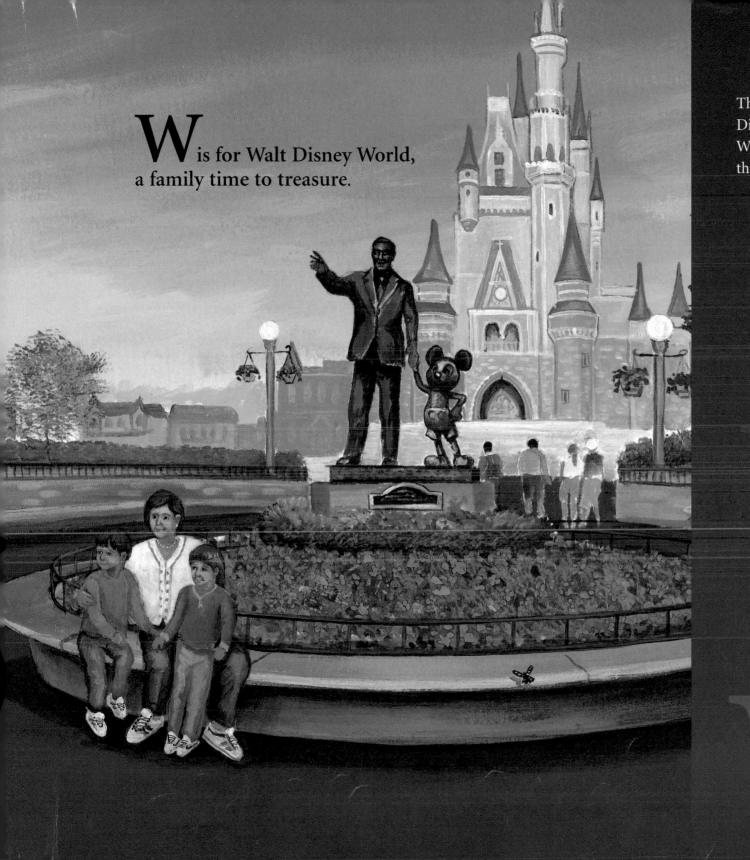

W is for Walt Disney World,
a family time to treasure.

There are many theme parks in Walt
Disney World, located in Orlando.
What fun for all families to enjoy, in
this great state of Florida.

The shape of the Horseshoe Crab looks like a horse's shoe. Its long tail is used as a rudder to steer the crab through mud. The tail is also useful in helping the crab flip itself, if a wave knocks it over on its back. This crab has four eyes, two on top of its shell and two on the front.

X is for Xiphosura,
a hard name to say.
Another name is Horseshoe Crab,
with tail and shell of gray.

COLUMBIA UNIVERSITY

KNOW ALL PERSONS BY THESE PRESENTS THAT

MARJORIE KINNAN RAWLINGS

HAS BEEN AWARDED

THE PULITZER PRIZE IN LITERATURE

FOR

NOVEL WRITING

IN WITNESS WHEREOF IT HAS CAUSED THIS CERTIFICATE TO BE
SIGNED BY THE PRESIDENT OF THE UNIVERSITY
AND ITS CORPORATE SEAL TO BE HERETO AFFIXED
ON THE NINTH DAY OF APRIL IN THE YEAR OF OUR LORD
NINETEEN HUNDRED AND THIRTY NINE

PRESIDE

Marjorie Kinnan Rawlings received
the Pulitzer Prize for writing *The
Yearling* in 1939. She lived on an
orange farm in Cross Creek, Florida.
The book tells the life of a family
working on a Florida farm. The
young boy in the story finds the joy
and sorrow of raising a fawn. The
book was later made into a movie.

Y is for *The Yearling*,
a prize book of local charm.
A boy, a pet fawn, and
life on a Florida farm.

Z is for the Zebra Longwing,
as pretty as can be.
She's flown across the alphabet,
from the letters A to Z.

The Zebra Longwing is the state butterfly of Florida. The largest butterfly house in United States, Butterfly World, is located in south Florida where thousands of butterflies exist in all stages of life. Butterfly World also has the largest Tropical Rain Forest Aviary in the world.

Z
z

A Shell Full of Facts

1. Do you know the city that is the lightning capitol of the world?

2. Name the river Stephen Foster made famous in the song "Old Folks at Home."
   This song was made Florida's state song in 1935.

3. Spanish moss gets its nourishment from what source?

4. Twice a year, Florida is plagued with what sticky bug?

5. Florida ranks first in what natural sweetener?

6. The bark of pine trees in northern Florida produces what product?

7. The Tamiami Trail connects two major cities. Can you name them?

8. What city is known as the "sponge capital of America"?

9. Black-eyed peas grew on the banks of what river?

10. What large river is one of the few rivers in the world to flow north?

11. Do you know the largest city in Florida?

12. What song was recorded on the world's first record?

13. Tabby is used in building walls. What is it made of?

14. By what name are tornadoes called along coastal communities?

15. Florida has two time zones; do you know what they are?

16. What portion of the Everglades is nearest the west coast?

17. The poisonous coral snake sports red, black, and yellow bands. What rhyme do you remember when telling the difference between it and a nonpoisonous king snake?

18. What is Florida's most valuable field crop?

19. Most of the state's oyster crop is cultivated in what town's ten thousand acres of oyster beds?

20. What bird has a beak bigger than his "bellican"?

Answers

1. Tampa
2. Suwannee River
3. The air
4. Lovebugs
5. Honey
6. Turpentine
7. Tampa, using the letters Ta, and Miami using the letters Miami; put them together and you have Tamiami.
8. Tarpon Springs
9. Peace River
10. St. John's River
11. Jacksonville
12. "Mary Had a Little Lamb" recorded by Thomas Alva Edison
13. Crushed shells, limestone, and sand
14. Waterspouts
15. Eastern and Central in the western part of the panhandle
16. Big Cypress Swamp
17. The rhyme to remember is "Red touch yellow, kill a fellow; red touch black, good for Jack."
18. Sugarcane
19. Apalachicola
20. Pelicans

Carol Crane

Carol Crane has worked for 25 years reviewing, lecturing, and enjoying children's literature. She is a respected national educational consultant, speaking at state reading conventions across the United States. Carol has opened up a new page in writing children's books that are fun to read as well as useful in the classroom. She lives with her husband Conrad in Bradenton, Florida.

Michael Glenn Monroe

Since a very young age, Michael Glenn Monroe has known that he wanted to be an artist. A self-taught painter, he spends much time meticulously honing his craft, often teaching himself new and unique techniques to add to his paintings. His realistic wildlife paintings have garnered him many honors throughout the years. Michael's other picture books include *M is for Mitten: A Michigan Alphabet*, *The Michigan Counting Book*, *Buzzy the bumblebee*, and *A Wish to be a Christmas Tree*, a book written by his wife, Colleen. They live in Brighton, Michigan with their twins, Matthew and Natalie.